My Mother and the Ceiling Dancers

Also by Zack Rogow

Poetry

Glimmerings
Make It Last
A Preview of the Dream
The Selfsame Planet
Greatest Hits: 1979–2001 (chapbook)
The Number Before Infinity

Plays

La Vie en Noir: The Art and Life of Léopold Sédar Senghor
Things I Didn't Know I Loved (a play about Nazim Hikmet)

Translations from the French

Earthlight by André Breton (cotranslated with Bill Zavatsky)
Arcanum 17 by André Breton
Horace by George Sand
Green Wheat by Colette
Marius by Marcel Pagnol

Children's Literature

Oranges

Anthologies Edited

The Face of Poetry with photographs by Margaretta K. Mitchell
TWO LINES: World Writing in Translation—Masks
TWO LINES: World Writing in Translation XIV

My Mother and the Ceiling Dancers

Zack Rogow

My Mother and the Ceiling Dancers
Zack Rogow
ISBN 1936715120
Kattywompus Press

Publisher's Position Statement on the Value of Poetry Arts

This book is a work of fine art from the poet

Zack Rogow

whose work you support for a few cents per page.
You are not buying paper and printer's ink by weight.
You selected language art that took as long to create
as paintings or other fine art. On behalf of a large
community of contemporary poets, this poet in
particular, independent and small press publishing, and
Kattywompus Press, thank you for supporting this project.

Kattywompus Press
2696 West Saint James Pkwy
Cleveland Heights, Ohio 44106
www.kattywompuspress.com

Acknowledgments

"A Western Window," *Full Circle*

"Across the Water," *Poetica*

"Airplane Tanka," co-winner, Tanka Splendor Award, 2006.
    Sections published in *American Tanka*; in
    *Bigger Than They Seem: Anthology of Very Short
    Poems*, Accents Publishing, 2011; and online.

"Evil Sex in French Cars," *Thirteen Hills*, Pushcart Prize-
    nominated

"First Trip Abroad," *Miller's Pond*

"French Quarter," *Pale House* & *Levure littéraire* online

"Gualala Beach," *Mercy of Tides: Poems for a Beach House*,
    Salt Marsh Pottery Press, 2003

"In the Eyes of the Stars," *Greatest Hits: 1979–2001*,
    Pudding House Publications, 2002

"Mums, We Called Her," *Chiron Review*

"New Year's Day: The Morning After," *Curbside Review*

"Portrait in a Landscape (Yosemite National Park),"
    Parthenon West Review, Pushcart Prize-nominated

"Sunday Morning Bernal Heights," *Mauvaise Graine 2*

"Symmetron: Sandcastles," *Zyzzyva*

"The Long Life Poetry Factory," *Seems*

"The Only Boy in Ballet Class," *Stoneboat*

I'd like to thank my publisher and editor, Sammy Greenspan
of Kattywompus Press, for her encouragement and wise
advice. I'd also like to thank the members of the Thirteen
Ways poetry group for their support and fine suggestions:
Idris Anderson, Beverly Burch, George Higgins, Diane
Kirsten-Martin, Scott Serkes, Melissa Stein, Lisa Gluskin
Stonestreet, Nancy Taylor, and Robert Thomas. I'm grateful
to Frank Paino for his critiques of some of these poems.

Contents

A Passion for Passion

French Quarter   1
Evil Sex in French Cars   2
Remember Paris   4
Pillow Talking   6

Mothers Are the Necessity of Invention

Across the Water   11
Mums, We Called Her   13
The Only Boy in Ballet Class   19
The Twitch in My Mother's Front Foot   21
Madonnas and Children   23

What Children Know

New Year's Day: The Morning After   29
Portrait in a Landscape (Yosemite National Park)   31
Symmetron: Sandcastles   32

The Map Alive

First Trip Abroad   36
Things Not to Say on an Airplane   38
Airplane Tanka   40

Treasure Hunt

Talking to Van Gogh's Ear   47
A Western Window   48
Gualala Beach   50
Terrestial EXTRA: Sea Ranch   51
In the Eyes of the Stars   52
Sunday Morning Bernal Heights   53
The Long Life Poetry Factory   54

Dedicated in loving memory
of my mother, Mildred "Mickey" Rogow

These poems celebrate her life
and values, as well as the reasons for living
that eluded her at points along her path.

A Passion for Passion

French Quarter

Wasn't that the dream that night on Bourbon Street
when we infiltrated a schmaltzy piano bar
in an old French blacksmith's forge
its walls still black from the blast of the fire
and the tipsy queen dressed head-to-toe in white
in a suit and boa
like the ghost of Tennessee Williams
gave you his river of feathers
coiling it over you
so you formed a double helix
around the lamppost on St. Philip
while you mugged for that shot

and didn't we literally
dance in the street that night
outside every Zydeco salsa Cajun fluorescent jazz bar
you swaying with that relaxed upward-glancing smile
till I knew this love would go nowhere
was completely impossible
without these moments
so incandescent
they melt down every pre-dawn doubt

Evil Sex in French Cars

Our passion left no step in love's progress untried, and if love itself could imagine any wonder as yet unknown, we discovered it. – Pierre Abelard, *The Story of a Calamity*

In high school we had a grammar book
most students loathed:
REVIEW TEXT IN FRENCH—THREE YEARS
but if you blacked out just the right white letters
you could make it read
EVIL SEX IN FRENCH CARS

Grammar is a taste
most detest but a few adore
like smelly cheeses
aged in caves
and fertile with flavor

or like the Allegory of Grammar
carved on the face of Our Lady of Chartres—
one student sleeps
head on desk
the other so intent on the professor's words
he can't stay seated

In the Middle Ages the faculty draped hoods
behind their backs
so students could tuck coins into their cowls
like sticking bills in strippers' bras

Crowds came to hear Pierre Abelard
describe how truth hovered
outside language
overturning the Sorbonne
till he locked eyes with his pupil Eloise

I wonder if he loved the flavor of her questions
and her mouth
and her folds
if he had to burrow
his finger in her and smear it on her nipple
till he could taste her sex
even on that most maternal spot

Some rules taste good to break
Some sentences insist on running on
long as cathedral naves
Others fragment like Chartres glass

Even the laws that govern
French irregular verbs
are more pattern than logic

In later life
alone in the monastery
Abelard dwelt
on the two live eggs they had ripped from his pants
He regretted his love
and the son they had named Astrolabe

but I wonder
if he also chewed on his most succulent memories
over and over
till he knew them
as well as his Latin conjugations—
even half a page away
the verb
he could still spot

Remember Paris

Remember Paris
how we followed the Seine at night
the sightseeing boats brushing their yellow floodlights
across the limestone houses

Remember each metro car
a talking map of the world

and how we climbed Montmartre
starting from the mini-carousel in *Amélie*
whirling its lights at dusk

Remember those
Modigliani nudes
that all looked like you

Musée d'Orsay
Musée du Louvre
Musée d'Art Moderne

Remember how you leaned over the edge
of the bathtub
and I entered you
like a swan

and the blushing
yogurts we ate for breakfast
with raspberry tarts filled with mascarpone
washed down with espresso

Remember the candy stores
with their multiflavored marshmallows
and slivers of lemon peel
hidden in black chocolate

When all our cat fights
kid tantrums
and missed messages add up to parting

Remember Paris
the Marais bistros
where even the squash and leeks glittered

the vendors under the plane trees
in the Jardin du Luxembourg
selling little paper bags of chestnuts
hot as torches

and the clipped street named for Olympe de Gouge
who first proposed a Declaration of the Rights of Women
and was guillotined

And don't you ever forget that flight attendant
who gave us the bottle of champagne
because we looked so sad
to be leaving Paris

Pillow Talking

The three years we lived six blocks apart
I searched for a way to sleep alone

Instead of pulling your back against me
I embraced the torso of a pillow
all through those long nights

One night at a time
the pillow changed

Slowly she turned into you
and kept me company
as I shielded her from loneliness

But there were some nights
I needed your real breathing so much
I'd wake at the hour
when fog moistened every surface
as if the whole street had cried
and no one was out except a few bar closers
and those with no pillow to go home to

Though I'm an atheist
I did thank God those nights
that my daughters never woke up
to find themselves in a fatherless apartment

And now that you and I finally share a bed again
I'm not used to your body
shifting in the night
this way and that
like a spring rushet

so instead of imagining that the pillow is you
I have to pretend
that you are my pillow

Mothers Are the Necessity of Invention

Across the Water

Lower East Side girl
every Sunday in the late 1920s
darted past the tenements
that seemed to have squished
two stories higher
they pressed so close.
And that brown-haired girl, my mother,
zigzagged down Delancey
dodging the pushcart vendors hawking
pickled green tomatoes and little pillow knishes.

The towers of the Williamsburg Bridge
opened their arms to her
as she walked across the water to visit her Grandma Tsippe,
who had come to America
just to live out the last few years of her life in peace.
Peace? In Brooklyn, would you believe?
Over steaming grains of kasha varnishka
Tsippe told the girl
about the domes of the churches of Kiev,
like bulbs of golden flowers,
and the glowing sand on the banks of the Dnieper.

My mother could see
that silver-haired Tsippe had been a beauty
so many years before
when her grandma was known for the high cheekbones
she passed down to my mom.

Family story—
those cheekbones took root
when the cossacks cornered Tsippe's mother

in front of her husband and children,
the ones they'd left alive.

And a wash of Tsippe's blood still swirls
in my veins, the fury
of the vanquished,

but that Tatar's blood
flows in me too, the blind
insistence of the conqueror.

Mums, We Called Her

In Memoriam: Mildred "Mickey" Rogow, 1919–1972

She'd tilt her head up in the mirror—
even before running out for a can of Campbell's—
to tweeze her questioning brows
and stroke mascara onto her black lashes
over those wrap-around hazel eyes.
After repainting her lips
with Cherries in Snow,
she'd fluff her dark waves
till she kindled.

As a teen in the Depression
she modeled in department stores,
pinwheeling in gowns high above 34th Street
in front of Park Avenue ladies
before she descended to the subway
that devoured its way
back to the South Bronx.

She learned to rumba
from the kids on the block
who aimed their Gothic radios at the street
on those summer days when the heat never stopped
leaning on New York.

She bragged of reading every volume of Proust
while on full scholarship at Washington Square College,
the Jewish campus of NYU in the 1930s.
Cornell offered to write her check, too,
but her purse didn't hold
even the train fare to Ithaca
and she feared the Ivy League country club
gates swinging shut in her face.

As a teenager she ran away from home,

tired of her father's steel rule
that no one could taste their food
till all the females had served him.
In college she even stopped signing her hated name—
Mildred—exchanged it
for an all-American totem, Mickey.

At NYU she smoked with the boys
in Greenwich Village, who rosined their pool cues
when they looked at her.
But thanks to a memory that snapped up textbooks
she still got her Phi Beta Kappa key—at age 19.
It always tinkled from her gold bracelet
(base metals gave her hives).

She followed her favorite economics professor
to a job in DC during World War II.
Singlehandedly she averted a funeral home strike
that would have wounded home-front morale.

She didn't fight to work
once the soldiers runnelled off returning ships.
I wonder—if she had been born a generation later
would she have written stories, novels?
She was the one
who helped me comb all the awkward phrases
out of my seventh-grade term paper
on Third Parties in American Politics.

A fascination for me,
since my mother hiked the neighborhood for signatures
for a strange character
called the Liberal Party,
founded to pull Jewish radicals
into the New Deal,
her ambivalent assimilation.
She had a lifelong love affair
with justice, marched across five decades

from the Spanish Republic
to the Black Panthers.

After the War she dropped her first husband—
a sweet, basset hound of a man,
and took up with my father,
whose former girlfriend, a recording artist,
married my mother's ex,
a love rectangle.

With my dad, Mums had that
spangle she'd hungered for
when her family had to run out at night
schlepping their suitcases
since they owed months on apartments
from Delancey Street to Harlem.
My dad had worn a captain's fancy
dress whites in the Navy.
Herman Wouk painted his *Caine Mutiny* hero
partly with him as model.

My dad wrote short stories and drama criticism
and Mums came with
when he reviewed opening nights.
After the last curtain
they sipped blue vermouth
with the stars at Sardi's
till the newsboys burst in with the early papers
and their verdict of hit or flop.

Seamstresses stitched for my mother
the clothes and bathing suits she sketched.
She dared the first bikini on Fire Island.
Once, on a trip to Capri,
she shook her head at the birdwomen
wearing *Vogue* clothing
and flaunted her loose pajamas
in a chic ristorante. No one dared comment.

But she never quite got back on her high heels
after my father went down in a plane crash.
That was the first time she tried it,
dragging mattresses into the kitchen
for me and my sister
while she twisted open the gas on the oven
without lighting it.
She called her first husband when she finally
shoved open the window.
He had to push greenbacks
into the doctor's bag
to buy his silence.

But thanks to a court fight and my father's insurance
she finally got that Park Avenue address.
It looked out on garlands of light
festooning East River bridges
that darkened suddenly
the night of the blackout
when my sister and I waited for Mums
by the dead phone.
We stared out over the metropolis
that went dark block by block
till she rushed up the seventeen flights to hug us.
She had great legs!

And she had a laugh so full
she got invited to tapings of live comedy albums
so it was hard to believe
that her ghosts had finally caught up to her.
She'd see them at night
"Dancing on the Ceiling."
Ella crooned that
slow tune while my mother dragged
on her filterless Pall Malls
and sipped thick tumblers
of Johnny Walker Red.
Did I crack it by accident,

that bottle of whiskey she handed me
to carry through customs?

On that flight back from Spain
she hemorrhaged tears,
the whole plane, it seemed,
watching. "Those fascist guardia,"
she spat, but now I look back
and also see the affair
with the tall American executive
that ended in Madrid
like the dream of a republic of equals.

Mums truly expected me to become president
so I could untangle all those wrongs
while she tanned in the reflected glory
like a Jewish Rose Kennedy.

Only later I learned
about the pills and the married men—
how she got through all those years
of being the only one responsible
for the key to our apartment.

After we left for college
Mums let all her hopes go out one by one.
She shut off the therapy
without telling anyone,
and soon after that,
stepped off the window ledge.

Mildred, Mickey, Mums:
for years and years I couldn't even look
at a photo of you, or live with any objects
you had owned,
till I realized you had slogged neck-deep in pain
for over a decade
to carry me and my sister

all the way to the end of childhood.

If only you had stayed alive
you would have gotten to hug
your four grandchildren,
who prove every day
that your beauty and brains still thrive
on this dangerous planet.

I wish I could have just one day back, Mums,
to feel your goodnight kisses
and to smell your face powder.

The Only Boy in Ballet Class

I know what you're thinking
but it's not about that.

It's about galaxies
of Austrian crystal dimming
as I shifted in my scratchy velvet seat.
The curtain was hiked up
and suddenly the pancaked dancers,
the costumes, and cut-out castles
beamed more real than daylight.

"Look how the cavalier partners her," my mother nudged
during the pas de deux.
The male launched the prima ballerina, letting her
fly. "Look how masculine he is,"
my mother admired.

I knew she was placing in my hands a message
about sex, about how to love a woman.

But when does the cavalier get to shine? I wondered.

Only when he soloed, it turned out. Then he
                               leaped into the music.
            Suspended.
Stretching time.

And my mother's message about the pas de deux
didn't mention where
a woman's desire was hiding,
like a lost continent.

So I began my life as a lover
with an obstructed view. Then

I dated a divorcée
who didn't believe
a woman's pleasure
just tags along after.
I started to carry the guilt
of all men for that deliberate ignorance,
while she taught me to play her cavalier.

I learned that dance well,
but still I had to find the man
behind the ballerina,
the one who only leaped
when the stage was empty.

The Twitch in My Mother's Front Foot

When my mother sat herself down
and crossed her legs,
she couldn't stay still,
her front foot kicked rhythmically,
like a prisoner
thrusting at a wall
with a secret chisel.

Why can't she stop that kicking?
I asked myself back then.
Why can't she order
her body to stop? I do,
and I'm a teenaged boy,
and it's not easy
to want a girl
so much
that my crotch inflates
when I'm sitting on a bus,
words curl up in my throat,
and street names for female nooks
sprout in my thoughts
till I wonder
if I've actually barked them out loud.

Now in my middle-age, my mother's kick
has taken up residence
in my own front foot. I catch
myself at it as I sit
through an edifying lecture
on translating a medieval French epic
into Norwegian.

I look around the room
and spy a couple of restless strangers

with the same rhythm
working their front leg,
and I recognize them:
comrades in arms,
guerrilla warriors
in the ragtag army
of passion.

Madonnas and Children

For three hundred years Italian artists
lovingly stroked layers of gesso, egg tempera, and oil
to create the madonna and child—
the mother presenting the baby
handing her breast to the infant
sealing the toddler's face to her cheek

Those male artists devoted their lives
to that warm seam
between mother and child
that no man
no matter how soft
can ever equal

the most basic of human activities
the inmost peel of all mammalian experience

Duccio, Giotto, Fra Angelico, Filippo Lippi, da Vinci

The mother modestly swaddled in many layers of black
with only the thinnest gold river
tracing the very edge of her demure garments

But then somewhere in the mid-fourteen hundreds
the madonna started looking hotter
her hair gradually poked out from her veils
and slowly curled
her midnight robes turned the colors
of a Tuscan sunrise
her gold halo evaporated from the center outward
and her features became as sinuous
as Florentine arches
in a makeover
that lasted centuries

and then just in the nick of history—
praise the Lord!—
rising from the water
fully nude
Botticelli's Venus

What Children Know

New Year's Day: The Morning After

Mylar confetti sparkles on the parquet
One balloon hovers near the floor
another pushes against the ceiling

Is it true everything is moving away from us
all the galaxies
always distancing
cousins
college friends
washed to the stretch points of the map

Today my kids go back to their mom's
after a week when they bounced in the snow
for the first time
for the first time surprised
by its complete absence of pigment
their boots gobbled by hungry drifts

The stars shift through the spectrum
Astronomers tell their speed from their color
their light waves bending like train whistles

Spreading throughout the house
confetti tribes people new rooms

What was it that chased the champagne
a mixture
of java
        Bailey's
                and whipped cream

On the way back from the mountain snow
everything disappeared in valley fog and rain
like an old poet's memories

except the red tail lights
                    ahead
                              glaring

But as my daughters and I glided down the highway
in our silver bubble
we formed the storm into poems

My twelve-year-old jotted down
"Rain is loud
it pounds on your ear
and creates a puddle of whish
that a car rushes through"

Together we listened
for those moments
when our Toyota flashed under an overpass
and the rain suddenly hushed

Portrait in a Landscape (Yosemite National Park)

Summer tourists photograph a ribbon of kids
or a squinting spouse
backdropped by gossamer water, but my daughter
snaps pictures of white trees.
Forest fire cleaned these trunks
of every needle,
every green cell.

In the car she rides shotgun
where her mother once sat,
before the tumors
burned through her body.

My daughter asks me to pull over at a turnout.
Aims at the bones of a tree.
Imagines an image
somewhere between
the tiny rectangle she holds
and this unembraceable panorama.
She frames a cascade of gnarl, pale
against resurgent underbrush.

Symmetron: Sandcastles

We knew the ocean
always won, our dribble towers on the beach
squibbling up and up like a Gaudi cathedral
cracked at sunset,
the sand escarpments rolled over
by a carpet of water,
and all our elaborate plan
of moats and seagull feather flags
crashed before the tide.

But it was a game we played with the tide,
loving how the waves kidnapped our flags
and streamed them off in the plan
of sparkles, seeing how long the water
waited till it flashed over
the chateaus we'd patted by the crown of sunset,
all of our cathedrals
eased to bumps on the beach,
the words our heels had etched erased gently by ocean.

The Map Alive

First Trip Abroad

At twelve, I had just woken up from the dream
of playing second base in Yankee pinstripes.
Anything
that breached my indifference
I resented. But my mother had wanderlust
so we packed
way too many bags and hat boxes
and rode the Great Circle
across Atlantic skies.

I was the burlap coal sack
my mother and sister had to lug
from Rembrandt to Rembrandt.
At first only strange money
interested me: half-crowns and guineas,
they still had farthings.

Then the first shock—the ceiling
of Westminster Abbey
splaying its lavish fans,
like a procession of limestone peacocks.
Hmm, I thought.

And how could I ignore those
iron jungles overgrowing the Metro entrances,
Notre Dame's stained-glass roulettes,
and a busty Victory
flying around the Louvre.

Venice floated into my dreams
even before I left it,
a blend of city, flotilla,
and wild party!
That Italian *gioia di vivere*

we tasted at every countless-course lunch
and in Michelangelo's
Goliath-sized David
naked in public. I loved how he defied
Friar Savonarola.

Spain, though. Spain
was still a prisoner of the 1930s,
guarded by Guardia Civil vultures
with their geometric hats
of patent leather.
The driver hated us Yankees for Franco
till the hill above Toledo.
Then the driver pointed
to the towers of the Alcazar and confessed
he'd been cornered there,
battling for his life and the Republic,
and my mother told him,
My friends, my friends, too.
He gave us sugar
to offer the giant gums of horses.

History gleamed
like a sword
with a mother-of-pearl hilt.
Now the map was alive
and I was in it.

Things Not to Say on an Airplane

So, when do we arrive in Somalia?

Is it all right if I do the safety demonstration instead of the flight attendants? I just need to borrow one of your uniforms for a few minutes.

Could I have a different headset? This one is swarming with millions of germs.

I really think I should be sitting in first class and they should be sitting here, don't you?

Excuse me, do you have any reefer you wouldn't mind sharing?

Then I'd rather you move to a different row now.

Once we're in interstellar space, may I take out my stun phaser?

I'll have the sparkling zebra blood. No ice, please.

And could I have about 113 of those little snack packages? I have a lot of hungry children at home.

I don't like any of the films you're showing. Would it be all right if I recited some of my poems to the whole cabin instead?

Hi, you don't know me but I know your mother. She told me you'd be on this flight and that you would give me your wallet.

Why are pilots always named Jim? Why do they always have Texas accents?

Don't you think it stinks how they just assign any old stranger to sit next to you, and you have no idea if they're crazy or dangerous or anything?

Flight attendant, you see that man three rows up? He's been listening to my thoughts. Could you ask him to stop, please?

I need that blanket you're all wrapped up in. You're not the only one who's cold, you know.

Thank you for talking to me, but I didn't really expect you'd be so weird. Here's a magazine. Please shut up.

Airplane Tanka

stranger sitting directly
across from me
waiting for the same plane
what life
are you returning to

tail lights flexing on and off
the jet climbs
the ramp of the sky
melting in seconds
into the fog

below the clouds
a hurricane tweezes
a coastline—
above the clouds
bright sun

why look for alien glyphs
in the grain?
so beautiful
the circles farmers plough
grooved like old records

across a rigid grid
of farmland
a river squiggles
unconcerned
with geometry

in that landscape
of neuron valleys
is there a single person
on those scratchy roads
who hears this plane I'm on

when his plane went down
suddenly
did my dad even have time
for last images
of me or my mom

a thin trail of clouds
goes on
for a whole county
rushing the ghosts
to their carnival

once deadly once
inking a whole region
the volcano
now in a cloud
bubblebath

I hurdle my neighbor
and head to the john
when it hits me I'm
walking way
above the clouds

these clouds streaming
all at the same
altitude—
boats
in a higher sea

the pure bliss of soaring
lighter than nitrogen
bores me now
put me back on the ground
where the real game is played

the plane snaps through
the cloudlayer—
the world
decides
to appear again

landing at home runway
dollhouses suddenly enlarge
or am I shrinking
to fit inside
their tiny doors

after the flight
one unclaimed suitcase
circles the carousel
after the flight one bag
doesn't arrive

Treasure Hunt

Talking to Van Gogh's Ear

I'm talking to you, Van Gogh's ear.
Are you the one
behind all his cinnabar
and viridian daring? How

could you have known
those sunflowers happy as brass,
that gorgeous medley of irises,
the cartwheeling constellations?

You were appended
to a burgundy explosion
masquerading as a head.
You were supposed to hear

bug-eyed assassins. Your job
was to make him paint shadows
ten times Rembrandt. How
did you know sunlight

so much brighter than the beams
that drape our portly sofas
and flash through the earrings
of our Murano chandeliers?

A Western Window

My whole life
I've never found the right chapel in a poem
where I can place my favorite word:
chryselephantine.
It means, "of gold and ivory"
and was minted in ancient times
to describe Hellenic figurines
whittled in ivory
with robes of gold.

The root burrows down to the Greek, *chrysos*,
meaning "gold," as in the chrysalis
a caterpillar jewels itself into
to grow the eyes on its wings;
and *elephas*—ivory,
a word that sailed all the way
from the pyramids on the Nile.

In the Middle Ages
Europeans exchanged their herb-cured olives
and cheeses of soft marble
for those curling tusks

to carve tiny diptychs
that seemed to teem
with damsels and pages and yeomen
no bigger than a fingernail.

But "chryselephantine" belongs
to a bygone time
when beauty was clutched
by the few and the mighty
instead of being diffused
into electrons

pattering screens of colored light
in hundreds of millions of homes.

Now satellites track numbered elephants
and the breast of the earth
has been gouged and gouged
seeking ores to smelt.

But I remember
Merovingian thrones
encrusted with ivory and gold
when the dipping sun flashes
on the western windows
of houses in the hills
across the bay.

Gualala Beach

tough wind
　　　　throws my voice
　back down my throat

waves mutter
as they shake themselves out
　　　　　against all that is stationary
　　their edges
　　heavy cream

　　　　　wild yellow
　　　poppies
　flutter on brittle
　　　orange
　　　cliffs

redwood driftwood
　　　　　smoothed and twisted
knee joint
of imaginary beast
　　　　　worm-eaten
　　　in reverse braille
　half-rune half
　　Japanese calligraphy
　　　　　what does it spell

Terrestial EXTRA: Sea Ranch

the waves prancing
        unspool
            billions
of micro-organisms
        that pull apart
            to reproduce
like Busby Berkeley
        chorus lines
            shot from above
linking into figures
        beyond human form
            the waves
ram their wings
        into rocks
            scattering a galaxy
of spray
        all the shapes
            of the universe
are here
        hiding somewhere
            on this planet

In the Eyes of the Stars

Does it all add up to zero
in the eyes of the distant stars—

our little kisses along the chin
our towers all eventually leaning
our mortal languages
the newest metaphors still hot as ingots
our bubbling planet cooling toward frost

In the eyes of the stars
our bodies
are mere transparent jelly
our loves
just a story
with chemical words

The stars with their dark sunglasses
gaze on the future demise of our species
impassive as gangsters

Or is it we
who point to the stars
and lap up their sparkle
knowing they also dazzle and die

Sunday Morning Bernal Heights

for Francine Slack, my freshman-year high school English teacher

Walking down from the crest of the hill
I glimpse the bay
fitting itself
snugly around the city.

A big black lab off-leash
bounds up
and shlurps my fingers.
"Maui," shouts the man behind him,
"stop that!" with a hint in his voice
that he knows there's no way
his dog will ever stop.

I buy bagels at the Good Life Grocery—
pumpernickel, onion,
everything. And lucky day!—
at the little latte shop I score
the last chocolate croissant for my daughter
with its tongue of dark flavor.

I pass a couple on the bench
in front of the Liberty Café,
the man weaving his arms together
to basket his baby
with its black lawn of hair,
an infant so new
the tags are just off,

and at that instant I know
I'm here to try to learn
how to cherish
all that will endure
long after I'm gone
and even what has not yet
passed through the membrane of being.

The Long Life Poetry Factory

I keep dropping my footprints onto the sand,
jogging just out of reach of the ocean's tongue,

trying to pile one more push-up
onto Saturday—switching

from low-fat to no-fat,
to tofu and tamari, tilting each night

a cup of heart-colored
wine—but why try

to live a long life?
Does it matter to anyone, even me?

Or will it just prolong the landscape's
dissolving like that distant

cliff that wraps itself
in a turban of mist? But

I'm a reader. I want to know the plot
before I'm buried in my plot,

how the years pull
the characters' faces

like a sculptor's thumbs.
I know the chapter I get

isn't the beginning, or the end,
or even the middle; and I know the tide

sometimes is so unspeakably sad
that the sky starts to melt,

but still I have to know
how the story comes out.

About the Author

Zack Rogow is a poet, playwright, editor, and translator. *My Mother and the Ceiling Dancers* is his seventh collection of poetry. His poems have appeared in a variety of magazines, from *American Poetry Review* to *Zyzzyva*. He is the editor of an anthology of U.S. poetry, *The Face of Poetry*, published by University of California Press. Currently he teaches in two graduate writing programs: the low-residency MFA at the University of Alaska, Anchorage; and the MFA at California College of the Arts. He lives in San Francisco.